D0149375

Hamsters
KW-015

Contents

Acknowledgements: I would like to thank Mr. and Mrs. Wade for their help in typing and checking the manuscript, and my wife for checking and selecting the photographs which were taken at my farm in Great Bookham, Surrey, England.

Photographers: Dr. Herbert R. Axelrod, Michael Gilroy, Ray Hanson, Burkhard Kahl, Harry Lacey, Penn-Plax, Mervin F. Roberts, Brian Seed, Sally Anne Thompson.

© Copyright 1989 by TFH Publications Inc.

Distributed in the UNITED STATES by T.F.H. Publications, Inc., One T.F.H. Plaza, Neptune City, NJ 07753; in CANADA to the Pet Trade by H & L Pet Supplies Inc., 27 Kingston Crescent, Kitchener, Ontario N2B 2T6; Rolf C. Hagen Ltd., 3225 Sartelon Street, Montreal 382 Quebec; in CANADA to the Book Trade by Macmillan of Canada (A Division of Canada Publishing Corporation), 164 Commander Boulevard, Agincourt, Ontario M1S 3C7; in ENGLAND by T.F.H. Publications Limited, Cliveden House/Priors Way/Bray, Maidenhead, Berkshire SL6 2HP, England; in AUSTRALIA AND THE SOUTH PACIFIC by T.F.H. (Australia) Pty. Ltd., Box 149, Brookvale 2100 N.S.W., Australia; in NEW ZEALAND by Ross Haines & Son, Ltd., 18 Monmouth Street, Grey Lynn, Auckland 2, New Zealand; in SINGAPORE AND MALAYSIA by MPH Distributors (S) Pte., Ltd., 601 Sims Drive, #03/07/21, Singapore 1438; in the PHILIPPINES by Bio-Research, 5 Lippay Street, San Lorenzo Village, Makati Rizal; in SOUTH AFRICA by Multipet Pty. Ltd., 30 Turners Avenue, Durban 4001. Published by T.F.H. Publications, Inc. Manufactured in the United States of America by T.F.H. Publications, Inc.

HAMSTERS

PERCY PARSLOW

Left: *Flesh-eared golden hamster in a typical eating position.* **Below:** *Beige hamster, a descendant from an original find in Syria in 1930.*

The Hamster

Little or nothing was known about the Golden Hamster until 1930. In that year, Mr. I. Aharoni, a professor of the Department of Zoology, Hebrew University, Jerusalem, was exploring an animal burrow near Aleppo, Syria. At the end of an eight-foot tunnel he came upon a mother with her twelve young ones, the first golden hamsters to be found alive in nearly a century.

This rare species was known as *Mesocricetus auratus*. This little family was taken to the Hebrew University. Some of the babies died during the journey and some died after their arrival at the university. Finally, only one male and two females survived. This trio was bred and became what we believe to be the source of every living golden hamster in captivity today.

The Hamster

In 1931, two pairs of descendants of these hamsters were sent to England where they were first bred by Dr. Hindle at Hampstead. Dr. Hindle sent some hamsters to the University of Glasgow and some to Regents Park Zoo. It was from these original hamsters that stock found its way into the hands of several breeders in the United Kingdom.

In 1938 golden hamsters arrived for the first time in the United States at the Public Health Service in Carville, Louisiana, where they were used for medical research. It was the research scientists who first noticed that hamsters made fine little pets. It was probably from the stock at Carville that hamsters became available to the public.

The golden or Syrian hamster, to give its correct name, is a delightful little pet. Its scientific name, *Mesocricetus auratus,* means middle-sized golden mouse. The name hamster comes from the German word *hamstern,* meaning to "hoard"; hoarding is one of the hamster's favorite habits.

The hamster is a fun, lovable pet that has continued to increase in popularity throughout the years.

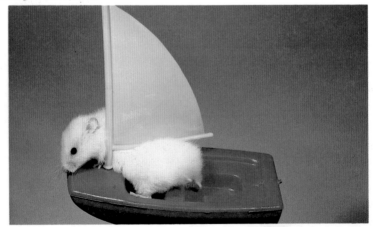

A golden hamster in the wild. The Syrian hamster is friendly and suitable for domestication, while some of its cousins are not.

The golden hamster, unlike its relation the European hamster, is usually tame, intelligent and friendly to humans. It is not so friendly to its own kind. Golden hamsters can be tamed with ease while the European hamster cannot be held, not even with gloves that have been re-inforced with steel mesh. The European hamster is about the size of the European wild rabbit. It is far from being a pet; in fact they are seldom—if ever—seen in captivity. They are fast moving and have a nasty bite. Fur coats made from the skins of European hamsters can be bought and are very costly. They tell me that the golden hamster cannot be skinned, so it is most unlikely that you would see a coat made from its skins. Since they have not been seen in the wild since 1930, I do not think that we have to worry about their being skinned for coats. The Djungarian hamsters (small desert or dwarf hamsters) make fluffy, cuddly pets. They are very pleasant to breed but occur only in the natural gray

Above: *The Chinese hamster has a dorsal streak of hair. It is smaller than the golden hamster and has a longer tail. This type of hamster makes an excellent pet.* **Opposite, top:** *Dwarf hamsters. Like the Chinese hamster, dwarf hamsters also have the black dorsal stripe, but unlike other hamsters, they turn white in winter to better camouflage themselves against the snow.* **Opposite, bottom:** *Normal golden or Syrian hamsters.*

The Hamster

color. The other hamster, the Chinese, is the same color as the Djungarian gray but has a black dorsal line. We do breed these, but their habits are not the same as those of the Syrian hamster.

Golden hamsters have always been found to be most obliging in captivity, being such clean, friendly, and inquisitive little darlings. They have most certainly made my life complete since their early days here. My wife says that I breathe, dream and think of little else but hamsters. I started the first hamster farm in the United Kingdom at Bookham, near Leatherhead, Surrey. In 1943 I was England's leading exhibition color breeder of hamsters, living then in Kingston on Thames in Surrey. My family has always been involved with animals and goes back in Kingston to the year 1600, according to a tombstone

Syrian hamsters are amusing and inquisitive animals, and they continue to appeal to more and more people.

A long-haired albino hamster. One of the challenges of keeping hamsters lies in the breeding of different color varieties.

in the local graveyard—that was before the Great Fire of London and the dreaded plague!

After we found that keeping large numbers of pets in a residential area was not, at times, in the best interests of both the animals and the humans, we decided to move right out into the country where we could breed just what animals we wished. We therefore found a nice bungalow with three acres of ground surrounded by four hundred and forty-seven acres of woodlands. The country air, the luscious abundance of green food and the peace and quiet all help to improve the quality of the pets that we now breed.

A side and rear view of a golden hamster filling its cheek pouches with food. As soon as its pouches are filled, it moves into a "secret hiding place" where it hides the food, much like a squirrel does. Keep this in mind when cleaning the cage. Too much stored food may bring unpleasant odors and insects.

Choosing Your Pet Hamster

Hamsters have become very popular as pets today. They are small, odorless, gentle, clean and easy to care for. They are very suitable as pets in small living quarters such as a bird cage or a small aquarium.

Hamsters are very entertaining little animals. They sit up, rest on their hind legs, climb and grasp anything that is within their reach. They enjoy doing acrobatic tricks; if you provide your pet hamster with an exercise wheel, he will probably run from four to eight miles each night on it.

Most pets require daily care and attention. Your pet hamster can be left alone for an entire weekend, if necessary, because hamsters hoard food and do not drink much. You will be fascinated to watch your hamster as it stuffs its food into its cheeks and then takes it out to hide it in special places in the cage.

Hamsters are very inexpensive to buy and to feed. They breed fairly easily. With enough care on your part, your hamster will be resistant to disease and will live out its lifespan of about 1000 days, almost three years. Some have been known to live even longer.

It is best that you buy your

When purchasing a hamster, be sure that the one you choose has a clean coat, bright eyes, and an interest in its surroundings.

A light gray tortoiseshell hamster. When it comes to hamster prices, the more fancy the variety, the more expensive the animal is.

Left: *Black-eyed white male hamster.* **Below:** *Black-eyed cream female hamster.* **Opposite, top:** *Cream satin hamster with a lovely, shiny coat.* **Opposite, bottom:** *Black banded hamsters.*

pet hamster when it is about five weeks old, after it has been weaned from its mother. If you buy one that is a year old or more, you will not have much time left to enjoy it. If you buy one that is under thirty days old, its body will be too immature for it to cope with its new surroundings. Again, five weeks is a good age for purchase.

When you buy your pet, it should weigh approximately an ounce and a half. Carefully observe its shape and general appearance for signs of good health—soft, silky fur, bright, prominent eyes. Lumps, bumps, discoloration, loose hair, wet bottom or tail, running nose or eyes, blood anywhere on the body and a nasty disposition are all signs that should steer you away from a hamster.

At the same time that you buy your hamster, you may also purchase a manufactured hamster cage in the pet shop. You do not, of course, have to buy one of these types—you may use a small aquarium fitted with a wire mesh screen top or even a strong parakeet cage. You could also fashion your own cage out of wood and wire mesh. Remember that the cage must provide privacy for sleeping and for hoarding. There must also be enough space for your hamster to use as its toilet area. You provide water, draft-free ventilation, and dry, warm cage litter. Wood shavings are the best materials to use for litter, but you may also use torn-up white paper towels. You should not place your hamster's cage in direct sunlight or in any bright light. Keep the cage in an area where the temperature is about 68° F.

Opposite: *In a clean, well-maintained environment, your pet hamster will thrive and provide you with hours of entertainment.*

This series of photos shows the actual mating of a pair of hamsters. The mating takes place very quickly. **Above:** *The light-colored male examines the female to be sure she will be receptive to his advances.* **Opposite, top:** *He then struggles to find the proper position for coitus.* **Opposite, bottom:** *Finally, he grasps her with his front paws and completes the reproductive act.*

Knowing Your Hamster

Your hamster's front paws are similar in construction to your own hand, so you must take care that no sharp objects are left for it to cut its tiny hands or fingers on. Hamsters use their little hands to fold food and bedding and to clean and wash themselves. Unlike a lot of little boys I know, they go to great trouble to keep themselves spotlessly clean. A cleaner pet you have yet to see, take it from me—I have kept hundreds of thousands of pets during my lifetime.

Hamsters are very fussy about their beds and will spend much time making a nest, only to move it again if they feel a draft.

Since hamsters are so clean in their habits and have no smell about them, they make ideal indoor pets, as many of us know already. They ask for very little—just a clean, draft-free cage and a simple diet—and they will require little more. Baby hamsters are not housebroken and will soil their cages anywhere. By the time they are about two months old they will have developed good, clean habits.

Hamsters have a strong sense of possession and feel

Below: *Hamsters require little more than a nutritious diet, a clean environment, and the love of their owner to live a happy and healthy life.* **Opposite:** *A young cream male Angora hamster.*

Above: *Hamsters are born naked.* **Below:** *As they grow older, they first grow hair, and then their eyes open.*

Above: *Female tortoiseshell hamster with her brood.* **Below:** *A black-eyed mother is shown with her babies.*

A black-eyed white hamster. The eyes make an interesting contrast with the coat.

that what is their property should not be disturbed. Unless you would like to have your hand nipped, do not intrude; keep your hands out of your hamster's nesting area and cage. Do not breathe heavily or blow on your hamster. A sure sign that it is annoyed with you will be that its ears are curled or laid back. This can often be seen when you first waken or disturb it. With a little patience on your part, its ears will soon uncurl and it will no longer be annoyed.

One hamster, one cage is the golden rule of housing for hamsters. Even pairs will fight and will kill each other. They will fight to the death if left together. When they are adults, the female will quite often injure the male and render him useless for breeding if they are left together longer than is required for a successful mating.

Like most young animals, your young hamster will be frightened of you at first. Hamsters are naturally friendly to humans and in a short while you and your pet will become accustomed to each other. Handled correctly from the start, your hamster will quickly become so tame that it will want to be fussed over and petted all the time.

I have found that the best time to start handling your hamster is in the early evening when the children return from school. Hamsters like human company and look forward to having a fuss made over them. Just tap gently on the cage and call your pet by name; soon it will learn to wake up when it hears its name being called. On no account should you try to pull it out of its bed while it is still asleep—this only makes hamsters cross and you will most likely have your fingers

A properly tamed hamster will love to get attention once it has become used to its new home.

Above: *These Chinese hamsters prefer a carrot to sunflower seeds.* **Opposite, top:** *A golden piebald hamster chews on a piece of green celery.* **Opposite, bottom:** *This hamster is unusual, as it has a white coat, yet has black ears and black feet.*

bitten.

As soon as your hamster wakes up it will run about, going first to its toilet area and then to the front of the cage to see who is outside. You can gently stroke it and in no time at all it will become accustomed to the smell of your hand. By the way, do not eat sweets or chocolate while you are handling your hamster. The smell will still be on your hands and your hamster might try to hoard your finger in its pouch, thinking that it is a piece of food.

Do not attempt to pick your pet up yet. Patience will be rewarded later. Just keep stroking it for a few minutes at

A trio of hamsters: a long-haired smoke pearl, a cinnamon piebald, and a yellow banded longhair.

When your hamster first wakes up, do not immediately take him out of his cage.

first and then offer a treat. Soon it will be taking food from your hands or fingers as confidence and trust in you grow.

Let your hamster walk out of the cage onto a piece of board or a piece of wire mesh at first. You should then let it walk back from the mesh into the cage where you have placed a little treat for it to eat. If you do this for a few evenings you will gain its confidence and it will allow you to stroke it while it is on the mesh. Gradually start to close your hand around its body. After a few days of this you will be able to lift your pet up from the board or mesh and return it to the cage, where you should have a little treat waiting for it. Afterwards you will have your hamster climbing into your hand and allowing you to stroke it gently.

Feeding Your Hamster

Quite a number of experiments have been made in both the United Kingdom and the United States on the feeding of hamsters that are used for research purposes, but very little has been done on the feeding of hamsters that are household pets. Over the years I have experimented in the feeding requirements and habits of the pet golden hamster.

One important factor I have found, at great cost to myself, is that severe diet change can and will upset your whole breeding program. About twelve years ago I thought it was a good idea not to have "all my eggs in one basket" in case there was an outbreak of a fatal disease. I started up another breeding establishment where most of the various colors would be bred. I

Below: *A satinized dominant spot hamster enjoying a few bites of watermelon.*
Opposite: *A good seed mixture will contain different types of seeds which provide the necessary nutritional elements. Pet shops offer a variety of brands from which to choose.*

35

Feeding Your Hamster

put a retired gentleman in charge of this colony; he had previously bred quite a number of small rodents and wanted to do something useful with his free time. It took about five years to get the colony going to a sensible breeding program and then I handed over the whole concern. Shortly afterwards we began having trouble and things began to go wrong. In a short time I found that the person who was feeding the hamsters kept changing their diet as the

supplies of the various foods changed. The stock was getting a continuous change in their diet; no sooner were they accustomed to being fed on a scalded dog biscuit, wheat, and flaked maize diet when it was changed to a diet of pellets, green food and water, etc. We soon put the stock back on a stable diet, one that did not change apart from a gradual increase in the amount of green food that was given daily.

It took several months before

A black-eyed white hamster investigating a seed cake.

Vegetables such as celery provide good nutrition and make nice snacks for hamsters.

we were back onto a steady increase in the condition, size and the general quality of the whole stock. Once back onto an even keel the litters grew larger and larger with very small losses.

Your stock can be changed over to a completely new type of food, but the changeover must be done slowly over a long period of time. I have found that hamsters will thrive on almost anything that man will live on—

except toffees, pickles and alcohol. Toffees will stick to the inside pouch and make your hamster dribble, pickles will kill your hamster and alcohol has killed more hamsters than it has revived.

Your hamster will be quite happy to be fed just once each day. The easiest times are in the evening when your pet wakes up or when the children come home from school. Hamsters are

Feeding Your Hamster

creatures of habit and become used to being fed at the same time each day. No two people agree on what the best hamster diet is, although hamsters will eat almost anything from fish and chips to rice pudding and custard. To keep your hamster in good health a well-balanced diet is a must.

I find that a diet consisting of food rich in protein such as lean meat, fish and eggs is very good; the protein intake should be at least one-seventh of the total food intake. Though cheese is a good source of protein, I would avoid feeding it because it causes smells.

For those keeping a large number of hamsters, a daily mash of scalded biscuit (small dog biscuit or biscuit meal), table scraps, some wheat, rabbit pellets, flaked maize and green foods or vegetables is quite suitable. If you do use mash, do not over-fill the feeder,

When feeding your hamster natural grasses or plant stalks, be sure that the plants have not been treated with chemicals of any kind.

Carrots are nutritious and are readily eaten by hamsters. This long-haired hamster is obviously enjoying this meal.

because mash turns sour very quickly and will smell up the cage. Grains—wheat, barley, canary seed, porridge and breakfast cereals, sunflower seeds, some bird seed and peanuts—mixed well and stored in an airtight container will make a good standby cereal mixture that will keep for weeks. If you feed this mixture along with added protein and plenty of green food (as much as your hamster will eat in twenty minutes), your pets will do quite well. You should not feed oats to your hamster, because the sharp ends tend to scratch the pouch and cause abscesses.

You can find packages of hamster food mixtures in most pet shops. The majority of these

Fresh, clean water must be available to the hamster at all times.

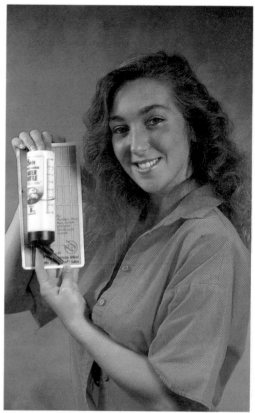

Pet shops offer different types of water bottles for hamster cages. Water bottles are more practical than dishes as they prevent the hamster from spilling water in his cage.

are quite suitable and reasonably priced.

Green foods will supply minerals as well as natural vitamins. They also prevent constipation, so all ages should be fed as much as they will eat. Hamsters especially enjoy such green foods as lettuce, cabbage (the outside leaves are the best), watercress, parsley, grass, dandelion (leaves only), chickweed, groundsel, clover (clover heads, too), trefoil and tarrow. In the winter I also feed my hamsters carrot, beetroot, swede, sweet apple, hawthorn berries and hawthorn leaves.

Never collect any green foods from places where dogs or cats visit—they may have urinated on the green food, making it poisonous. Poisonous plants such as deadly nightshade, henbane, oak leaves, buttercups, laurel leaves and hemlock should be kept away from all pets.

Baby hamsters love to scramble about the nest finding fresh green food. It is a good idea to cut up a mixture of green foods and sprinkle it around the nest. Both babies and mother will relish this little treat. While your hamster will enjoy a little bit of sweet apple, all citrus fruits should be avoided.

Your hamsters should have access to fresh water at all times. When a mother is rearing her litter, fresh water is a must. When your hamster is eating moist mash or feeding on fresh green food it will drink very little: nevertheless, it is a good policy to keep fresh drinking water available should it want it. Water is best given in the drinking bottles that are sold in most pet shops. Drinking water that is kept in open bowls is sometimes fouled by your hamster. Your hamster can drink milk, but this can turn sour in the hot weather;

Left: *A variety of food dishes can be found in your local pet shop. Check the size of your hamster's cage before selecting such a dish.* **Opposite:** *Fruits make nutritious treats for hamsters, but be sure that they are not given too often, as an excess can cause intestinal problems.*

again, it is best to use a drinking bottle.

Water is a must for pregnant or nursing females. A special diet is not required at this time, but starchy foods should be avoided because they cause fatness. The fatness could cause dystocia (inability to give normal birth).

When the babies are about nine days old, sprinkle wheat germ around the nest with the green foods that I mentioned above; the babies will thoroughly enjoy this very healthful treat. Stabilized wheat germ meal is sold under many brand names for humans in drugstores, supermarkets and health food stores.

You will be amazed at the energy the babies will have at about ten days old, so make certain that you make enough of the sprinkle mixture for the whole litter and for the mother too or else the biggest in the litter will eat all the mixture, even if it means fighting for it.

Care in feeding correctly while your hamsters are young will show up later, so take care that you do not feed any of them fattening tidbits.

Other noteworthy facts that I should mention here are that you should keep all foods stored in lidded containers to avoid having them spoiled by contamination from other pets or animals.

Hamsters can be kept safely in grammar schools if care is taken to provide plenty of water and food, especially carrots or root vegetables that contain a lot of moisture.

Also, the use of swede, carrot or beetroot should be avoided if you are breeding white hamsters for showing, because these foods can discolor the fur or hair.

Opposite: *The best way to keep one's hamster healthy and well nourished is to feed it a variety of different foods.*

Housing Your Hamster

Hamsters are naturally curious and fun-loving. They will investigate anything that is within their reach.

The "golden rule" of one hamster to one cage cannot be over-expressed. Therefore, if you are keeping just one hamster or thousands you must give special thought to the cages that you will be using. Since there are not many rodents that I have not kept at one time or another, cages have never been a problem for me.

You can use home-made wooden cages, but you must remember that your hamster can gnaw through almost any type of wood that you might choose to use. Of course, your hamster would take great delight in gnawing through its cage; your delight would not be so great when you find that your pet has escaped. If you had other hamsters in cages and the escapee tried to walk across their cages it could lose its feet. A hamster cannot bear other

Opposite: *A young rust female and a dominant spot male. Male and female hamsters should be kept in separate cages once they have reached the age of four to five weeks.*

hamsters, mice, dogs, noses or fingers places on top or into its cage. To give you an idea as to what could happen, if you were to poke a stick of chalk through an opening of the cage the hamster could bite right through it with one snap of its teeth.

To avoid having the cage gnawed, all wooden surfaces should be covered with wire mesh—I found this to be most satisfactory when I used wooden cages. I later switched to metal cages, but these, because they rust and corrode, were too costly to maintain in the large numbers that I needed. About five years ago I switched to plastic cages because they are easier to handle, are non-corrosive, non-absorbent, light and easier to keep clean and sterile. This type of cage is used mainly in research laboratories. These cages are inexpensive and they last quite a long time—ten times longer than the wooden or metal cages. Aquariums also are excellent when adapted to use as hamster homes.

The size that we use for a

Hamsters will enjoy playing with toys and cage furnishings, but be sure that their cages do not become too crowded.

An interesting variety of cage furnishings can be found in your local pet shop.

mother and her young is approximately 45.72 cm by 30.48 cm by 20.32 cm deep (18 in. x 12 in. x 8 in.). This height seems to be quite good, making the cage draft-proof and allowing the hamster to get plenty of exercise from walking upside down on the wire mesh top (they delight in doing this). Since this cage is not too high, should your hamster fall from the top it would not be hurt when it hits the sawdust on the bottom of the cage. The idea of letting your hamster use the top of the cage in this way doubles the walking area of the cage and keeps it fit.

Cages can be kept in tidy order, clean and well ventilated.

Hamsters occasionally like to stretch out and stand on their hind legs.

In the early days I tried keeping my cages on shelves but I found that the shelves warped with age and with the heavy cages on them. The shelves were also bad because they stopped the free circulation of air which is necessary for the animals that are kept in the cages.

To make the racking is quite simple. Start by using 1" by 2" lumber for crossbearers. The whole racking can be nailed or screwed together and made almost any size and height to suit your building. An additional advantage is that this type of fixture can be added to when extra racking is required. If you make a slight slope towards the back you will help stop the cages from creeping forward by the vibrations that the hamsters make.

The racking should be spaced to suit the size of the cages that are being used. You may buy those that are used for research purposes. You could also use an old aquarium made of glass or clear plastic. A tight-fitting lid made with a wire mesh insert will do the job well. This type of cage is very good for use in grammar schools because it is clean and tidy and the children will be able to see the hamster at work or at play without trying to put their little fingers inside the cage. I prefer the plastic tanks to the glass because the glass is very cold and does cause condensation to run down the sides of the cage.

Ladders are one of the hamster's favorite toys; going up and down will amuse them for long periods of time.

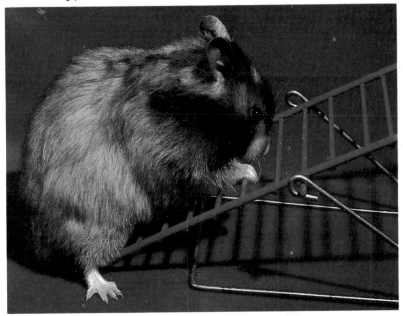

Left: *Cedar is just one of the many types of cage bedding available at your local pet shop.* **Opposite:** *A rust hamster.*

Unless ladders or other playthings are placed inside, the hamster will stay on the floor and will not be able to reach the top at all. Do not forget that hamsters are natural burrowers. When I see some of the hamster cages that are on the market I often wonder if the makers think that hamsters are able to fly. As hamsters are short-sighted—the distance they can see being approximately nine inches (22.86 cm)—why make high cages that can cause a fall and injure your hamster?

So many people have the idea that animals think as we do—they do not! In fact, I often think that they are far more intelligent than the humans who are trying to care for them. To fill pet cages with nest boxes, ladders, toys and a lot of odds

Most hamsters of the same sex will get along with each other. If a fight seems imminent, however, quickly separate the animals and keep them in separate cages.

and ends may give pleasure to the owner but not to the pet. The fact that these unwanted objects restrict the pet's movements is seldom thought of. The owner also does not think of the possible injury that their hamsters may face with all of the things left inside the cage.

A water dispenser and a small heavy pot for its food within reach are essential. For a nesting place, why not let your hamster choose this for itself? After all, if it does not like the spot that you might choose, it will move the bed anyway. Your hamster will choose a place that is out of the draft, even if it has to move the nest time and time

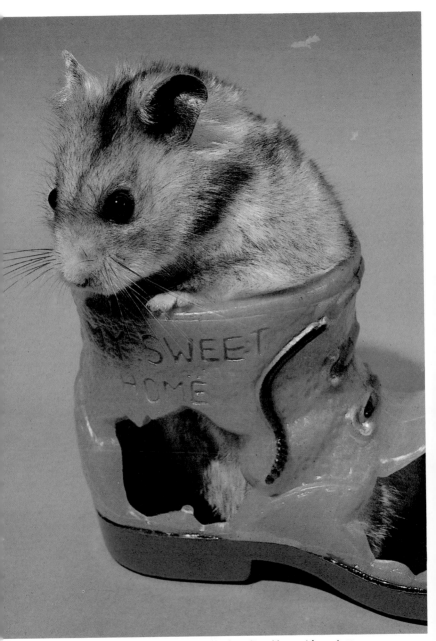

Shoes, whether real or hamster-size, are a favorite with most hamsters.

Housing Your Hamster

again before finding the best place. I have found that hamsters will make the nest away from sunlight, away from an open window ventilator and away from floor drafts that we are unable to notice.

White pine or cedar chips are best to use for floor covering. On no account should you use newspaper, because the print is poisonous. About one inch of sawdust is suitable; if more is used, your hamster will only push it out trying to stop noises or drafts from entering the cage. For bedding use white paper towel cuttings; being clean, white and fresh-smelling, they do the job well and you will not need to

Hamster in a standard British exhibition cage. This cage is too small for everyday housing.

Hamsters will select a certain spot in the cage where they will hoard their food. Sometimes this place will be under a favorite toy.

worry about your hamster eating them. There are quite a number of so-called hamster beddings offered for sale, but beware of any that are fluffy, like cotton wool. Cotton wool has been found to have caused a lot of deaths by blocking the gut of hamsters when it is swallowed. I have also seen fiberglass, felt, aquarium filter, kapok, and various other types of bedding; do not use any of these, because they mean certain death for hamsters. Get the type of bedding used by your pet dealer for his hamsters.

Good, clean, soft meadow hay is far better to use as bedding than most materials. The only reason that we do not use hay is that it may have been visited by cats, dogs, rats, squirrels, birds or any other animals that may be carrying fleas and lice. Hay that has been subjected to urine from such animals is fatal to hamsters.

Breeding

Above: *A satinized chocolate and white female hamster.* **Opposite:** *A young gray satin female hamster.*

Before you attempt to start any breeding program it is best to make sure of a few things: 1) How many hamsters can you care for? Remember, only one hamster to a cage. 2) Where are you going to keep your breeding stock? Breeding stock must be kept at a steady temperature, not in a place that might have a rise and a fall of ten degrees or so. The breeding stock needs a quiet place where there will be little disturbance, a place where they will not be troubled by vermin and a place that is easily kept clean.

Make sure that the building is escape-proof; even the best breeders have hamsters that escape. Should a hamster get loose and run over a cage in which there is a mother and babies, the mother may attack her own babies out of fright.

I will mention a few places

that are good for breeding. A spare room is ideal, if fitted with an exhaust fan; an outside brick building is good, as is a well-insulated wooden building with windows and an exhaust fan.

A garage is not very suitable if you use it to park your car in; car noises and gas fumes are fatal in the breeding pen. Greenhouses or extensions that are made with a lot of glass are not suitable because there is a constant temperature change there.

After you have decided on

When you bring your hamster home, gradually get him used to his new surroundings and to being handled. In time, he will grow to love the attention you give him.

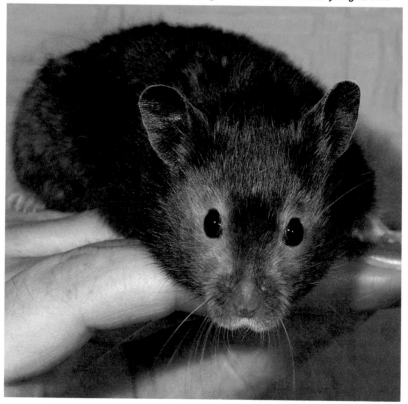

A group of young female hamsters. It is imperative for a breeder to keep accurate records if he is to produce quality, properly bred animals.

where you are going to keep your breeding stock, you must decide on how many you can handle and on the type of cages that you are going to use. Do not forget to keep a few extra cages on hand in case you have an emergency.

When choosing your breeding stock always use the best you can obtain. If you are going to color breed, it is all important that you start off with purebred stock. If your initial stock is of poor quality then all the clever feeding, breeding, fancy diets or super housing will never give good results. Breed only from stock that you know is good— choose your parent stock carefully, bearing in mind the litters they come from. Always keep records of your breeding in a book or on a chart on a wall. Such records should show parentage, date of mating, date due, number of young born, number of young reared, sex, color and any mis-matings. Some fanciers keep record cards on each cage. This is satisfactory unless a hamster gets out and chews them up. By keeping complete records you can build up a reliable strain. Show qualities can be built up and passed on only if you know the history of your breeding stock.

The males used for breeding should be selected for color, type, size and parent fertility. Some males are unable to sire good litters and if your records show this, you should get rid of them and keep only the best. It has been proven that it costs more to keep a bad animal than a good one, and since you will be keeping one male to about ten females, each male that you have must be a good one; if not, you could have ten females

A family of golden hamsters in the wild. Young hamsters should be removed from their mother's nest at about three weeks of age. By then, they should have been properly weaned.

A litter of one-week-old long-haired hamsters.

producing lots of poor males.

A healthy female will rear litters of ten or so with little trouble if she is ten to twelve weeks old when you first mate her. To maintain stamina in your stock it is best not to use them for breeding before this age; your females will more than likely produce small litters of runty youngsters if you mate them younger. Breed only from mature stock and you will not regret it in the long run.

Females will mate again when the youngsters are 28 days old but, again, better results are obtained if the mother is given more time, about two weeks, to build herself up. Rearing a litter pulls down the mother at the best of times. Four litters from a good mother is my aim; after this they cannot be relied upon.

Breeding

The stud males can also be used too often. I like to allow about four days between matings. I find this keeps the male in good breeding condition. After about fifteen months your male will look old—and will *be* old—and I advise replacing him at about a year old. One old chap I had years ago lived to be seven years old and was fertile. He sired litters at four years old, but he was one in thousands!

Females will mate when they are "in season" or "in heat" as it is often called, which is every

A mother hamster with her two-week-old litter.

A group of young black-eyed cream and cream banded hamsters.

Above: *A nice pink hamster.* **Below:** *Two tortoiseshell and whites and one gray hamster.*

Above: *An adult gray hamster.* **Below:** *A young, immature gray hamster.*

Breeding

four to five days. The usual time for the female to come in season during the winter months is during the hours of darkness, but during the hot summer they come in season much earlier and for a longer time. I have had successful matings early in the morning during nice hot days.

A wooden box about 30.48 cm (12 in.) square with a wire mesh top I have found best for mating purposes. A clean pen or an empty cage (without sawdust or bedding) could also be used with success. Mating hamsters on a table top is out of the question, as quite often, when the female decides she has had enough, she will turn on the male. To avoid her I have seen the male jump into the air and land on the floor, hurting himself badly. If the female is not in heat she will soon attack the male and should be removed at once

A long-haired cinnamon hamster.

A cinnamon dominant spot female hamster. Females selected for breeding must be in excellent condition if they are to produce quality babies.

before she does any damage to him. If left in with him she could quite easily render the male unable to sire any further litters.

There is no reliable way of telling when the female will be in heat except by trying each and every night for about ten days. As soon as the female is in condition and ready to mate she will stand rigidly waiting for the male, with legs outstretched, tail high; nothing else in the world will seem to matter to her. The male will visit her repeatedly for about twenty minutes. The pair should then be parted and returned to their separate cages.

It is not easy to part fighting hamsters, but it is a help to change the smell by sprinkling sawdust that smells of disinfectant over them. As soon as they break away, a piece of cardboard or a paint brush will keep them apart. Just why they do not like brushes I cannot say, but the fact is that they do not.

Above: *Flesh-eared albino males, one longhair, the other normal.* **Opposite, top:** *A golden piebald hamster.* **Opposite, bottom:** *A cinnamon banded hamster.*

Try sweeping the floor near their cage with a broom and they will swear at you instantly—maybe a brush sounds like a snake hissing?

So called "check-mating" is a waste of time; it is not a check for pregnancy. I have found that even when pregnant, female hamsters will stand for and accept the male up to four days before the litter is due. It is better to wait ten to twelve days than to have your female abort. If the female is too fat she will not mate at all. It is most common for some breeders to blame their hamsters for being too fat when it is actually their own fault for allowing the animals to get too fat. To help virility, vitamin E, found in green food, should be fed before attempting to mate.

Should the female rub her rear on the floor when put to the male, remove her at once, as this is her way of distracting the male's attentions. When doing this she is giving off an offensive fluid which is very unpleasant indeed.

The gestation period is sixteen days (shorter than a mouse, rat and other rodents). Before the female is due to have the litter, check her cage, making sure everything is nice and clean with fresh bedding added. This job should be done about four days before the kindling date— not later. Do not start poking about in the nest as soon as the litter is born—leave well enough alone; any disturbance could result in the mother destroying the babies through fright. Just carry on with the usual feeding, etc., until the babies are about fourteen days old before cleaning out the cage. The babies will be born naked and blind but will grow at an amazing rate if left undisturbed; of course, you must eventually supply them with food, milk and water. At seven days they will be growing fur and will not be colored pink anymore, unless they are white ones. The babies will start to leave the nest at around ten days and move about outside the nest; their eyes will be fully open at twelve days old. At this age you will find that they require lots more food; the amount they will consume will be enormous. When about 24 to 28 days old the youngsters should be taken away from the mother. After 28 days a female in good condition might turn on the babies, so make sure they are away from her so this will not happen. Two cages are required for the newly weaned youngsters. Put the males in one and the females in the other. By doing this right away you will avoid any possibility of brother and sister mating; it also cuts down the chances of torn ears and faces. Before the youngsters are six weeks old you will have had plenty of time to select those

required for your own future breeding stock; they should be caged separately. Find good homes for those not required.

A dove female and a long-haired lilac male. These hamsters are sniffing, a preamble to mating.

Above: *Black-eyed cream and a ruby-eyed cream hamster.* **Below:** *A mother and her litter of black-eyed creams.*

Above: *A golden banded hamster.* **Below:** *A long-haired cinnamon hamster.*

Sexing

It is very easy to tell the sex of hamsters. At a very early age you can see two rows of seven mammae spots or teats on the female if you hold her at arm's length. The body of the female is rounded off at the rear while the male has an extended rear with a bulge under the tail where the testes are concealed. During the hot summer months they often become enlarged and appear red or mauve and are very pronounced. This is quite normal and is nothing to get worried about. Both youngsters and adults can be sexed quite easily by examining the sex organs and their position. On the female the vagina is very close to the anus while the penis is much farther away on the male.

Below: *When determining the sex of a hamster for the first time, it is wise to get the help of an experienced breeder or veterinarian.* **Opposite:** *A young cream angora female.*

Above: *A satin black-eyed white hamster.* **Below:** *A satin yellow hamster.*

Above: *A satin cream hamster.* **Below:** *A pair of hamsters inspecting one another to become acquainted*

Color Breeding

Color, color, and still more color is something that I am known for. Quite a number of new-colored hamsters started life with me over the years, being made up from other color combinations. Before going into any color-breeding program you must be sure that the stock that you will be using is true to color or, to put it another way, pure. A reputable breeder would be using only true-bred stock to keep his own stock going.

If you mate a golden to a cream all the youngsters would look like goldens to the inexperienced. To be more exact, they would be F1s or youngsters from the first crossmating. They would be carriers, that is, carrying one color but looking like another. They are really a combination of two colors even though the cream color seems to have disappeared. In this case the F1s are goldens split for cream. If one of this generation is mated back to a pure cream the next litter would be made up of approximately one-half goldens and one-half creams. If two of the F1s were mated together the results that you should expect would be three times as many goldens as creams in the litter. It has been proved that any two of the creams from this mating (F2) would produce their like, all the litter being cream.

Similarly, if a golden were mated to any of the following colors in the same way the same pattern of inheritance of colors would happen—sepia, dark-eyed albino, piebald, honey, cream red-eyed, cinnamon, albino. This inheritance pattern, however, does not occur when mating white band or white bellied stock. The mating of white band to any self color would give approximately half self color and half banded in each litter. The same proportion would also occur when mating white belly to self color. Today many hamsters sold have been cross-bred or are split animals. It is of great importance before coming to conclusions to make sure that your initial stock is pure. It is useless to attempt to breed new colors from cross-bred stock; and similarly, to try to produce good breeding stock from such cross-breeds is a waste of time and energy. The results obtained could vary in each and every litter.

So many times I hear breeders' tales of how they mated a golden to a white and

Opposite: *A black-eyed white hamster, a strain which was bred from the dominant spot and cream varieties.*

Above: *A long-haired golden piebald hamster.* **Below:** *A long-haired albino hamster.*

Above: *A satin tortoiseshell and white hamster.* **Below:** *A mosaic black-eyed white hamster.*

the resultant litter produced creams, whites, goldens and other colors. They appear so astonished when I say they did not. What they did not realize was that one or both of the parents were carriers—in fact, both parents must have been carriers of all of the odd colors that were produced.

One hamster could be crossed or split to any number of colors since it is easy to put the color in; it is very difficult to take the color out. If, for example, you mate a golden to a cinnamon and you get a litter of goldens and cinnamons, then it can be assumed that the so-called golden was split for cinnamon.

A satinized cinnamon female hamster. Satin hamsters continue to grow in popularity, especially the different color varieties.

A pregnant satinized cream banded female hamster.

Whereas, if you mate a golden to a golden and the litter consists of both golden and cream, it is proof that both the goldens were carriers of cream.

The white-bellied hamster—a permanent carrier of the eyeless gene—can be detected by the overwhite (brighter than white) belly fur. The black-eyed white is a carrier of the eyeless gene, so to avoid this eyeless trait, you should mate a black-eyed cream to a black-eyed white. The resulting litter would consist of about half black-eyed whites and half black-eyed creams but the eyeless gene would still be present in the litter.

A strange mating is that of a cream banded to a black-eyed white. The litter would be half black-eyed whites (self color and banded) and half black-eyed creams (self color and banded). You could see the banded creams, but not the banded whites, since a white band

Opposite: *A long-haired cinnamon cream hamster.* **Above:** *A golden banded dominant spot female hamster.* **Below:** *A tortoiseshell female hamster. The tortoiseshell coloration is sex linked and sex limited; thus, it is found only in females.*

cannot be seen on a white hamster. Nevertheless, if you mate all of these black-eyed whites together, you would find in the litters eyeless whites, black-eyed creams, black-eyed cream bands and black-eyed whites with bands of white which, although present, cannot be seen.

Ruby-eyed stock can only be produced from ruby-eyed stock. To be more precise, it can only be produced from ruby-eyed females being mated to stock carrying the ruby-eye gene. As all ruby eyed males are sterile (I have proved this over the last 28 years), the males used for this purpose must be carriers of ruby-eye, or F1 ruby-eye stock. Mate a black-eyed cream to a ruby-eyed cream female and all the youngsters in the litter will carry the ruby-eye gene. From these, select the best pair and mate them together. There should be at least one ruby-eyed

A fawn female hamster.

A good diet is important to all hamsters, but especially to hamsters that are to be bred, whether they are male or female.

cream or fawn in the litter resulting from this mating.

To continue mating ruby-eyed creams: mate two of the creams together. To breed ruby-eyed fawns, mate two of the split goldens together. To create a ruby-eyed cream band: mate a black-eyed cream banded male to a ruby-eyed cream female— the young will all be black-eyed creams, some with a band and some without. One of those young males (with the best band) should be mated to any other

ruby-eyed cream female; the offspring from this mating will be black-eyed creams and black-eyed bands, ruby-eyed creams and ruby-eyed cream bands. Only males carrying the ruby eye (split for ruby-eye) can be used since all of the males that show a ruby eye will be sterile. Continue in this way until the litters produce all ruby-eyed youngsters.

Using similar methods you can produce colored long-haired stock. By mating a normal-

Above: *A scrawny, pet quality female hamster searching for an escape route.* **Opposite:** *An extremely long-haired hamster which descended from the same wild hamster type.*

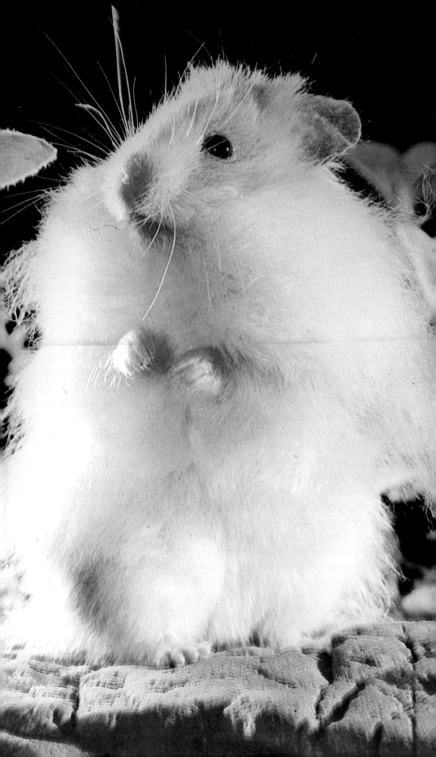

coated stock to a long-haired stock the young will be carrying the long-hair gene. By mating two of the F1 litters together, long-haired youngsters can be produced. Combining this with the colors required, it is possible to breed all of the colors with long hair and they will continue to produce long-haired youngsters.

Again, using this same method you can breed all the colors in your stock with satin coats. By mating a satin-coated hamster instead of a normal-coated one to any of the matings that I have suggested in this book, litters of half satin and half normal coats will result. For instance, mating a black-eyed cream to a satin black-eyed cream banded would give a litter of both cream and cream banded. If one of the parents were a satin then half of the entire litter would be satin; some would be satin cream and some would be satin cream banded.

How about breeding a satinized, long-haired, banded cream mosaic? It can be done in the same way; we have several at this time. Perhaps you would prefer a long-haired, satinized tortoiseshell and white piebald hamster? Have a go at it—you can do it from scratch in about two years.

BREEDING FACTS

Mating times:	between 22.00 and 24.00 hours
First mating:	between 12 and 14 weeks
Oestrus cycle:	between 4 and 5 days
Gestation period:	16 days average
Average litter:	6 to 7
Eyes open:	10 to 12 days
Separate caging:	between 24 and 28 days
Life expectancy:	18 months
Maximum age recorded:	3 years (7 exceptional)
Breeding age:	3½ to 4 months
Age of puberty:	male—60 days, female—60 days
Weaning age:	21 days
Body temperature:	97.2 to 99.5° F
Breathing rate:	average 75 breaths per minute
Heartbeat:	375 to 400 beats per minute
Daily food intake:	10 to 15 grams
Daily water intake:	15 to 20 milliliters
Daily urinary volume:	max. 12 milliliters

A golden dominant spot female.

A family of golden hamsters.

Purchasing Stock

My idea on this subject has always been that you should buy the best that you can from the best breeder that you can find. It costs far less to keep a good quality hamster, or any other pet for that matter. If possible, buy from a well known breeder-exhibitor who you will be able to trust. After all, his good name in the Fancy is at stake and he is not likely to do anything to damage his reputation. To risk losing his good name among fellow fanciers or losing his good standing at club meetings or at shows open to the public would be out of the question for any reputable breeder.

If you do not know a good hamster then ask the breeder—he will help you. Remember, the hamster that he sells to you may be in a show together with many other hamsters that had been sold by other breeders; if yours is a poor one, everyone at the show will see it. A good breeder would not take the chance of selling you a poor specimen.

If it is a pet that you want, there are a number of club members who breed a few good ones but cannot keep them all for themselves. Some of these hamsters may find their way into local pet shops. If kept in good condition at the shop, these would suit you very well. You would not expect to be buying

Below: *When purchasing hamster stock of a particular variety, try to find the best quality animals you can.* **Opposite:** *The closer a particular animal is to the standard (for its variety), the more expensive it will be.*

Purchasing Stock

the best since the breeder keeps the best for himself; there is no reason why the others cannot be good as pets. Beware of the shop that keeps both sexes in one cage. How horrified you would be if you found that the baby hamster you have is about to have a family—probably sired by its brother! A good retailer would offer stock that has been separated by sex and sold at about 24 to 28 days old, when they would not be pregnant.

Beware of those shops selling youngsters bred for research purposes—this type of stock is usually mass-produced, in-bred and not handled, in which case they would not make good pets. A breeder in the hamster fancy is pleased to handle his stock as much as he can. One of the reasons I changed from men to young lady assistants was because young ladies love to handle the young animals and make pets of them. Although we breed some two hundred and fifty each day, some of the staff still call the mothers by name when feeding them.

If possible, why not visit a hamster farm and choose your own hamster? There are breeders who offer to ship stock of your choice and guarantee live and safe delivery, so why not have one sent to you? Hamsters are sent from my farm all over the world and arrive in perfect condition. Only a few years ago I sent 24 pregnant females to Jamaica, a journey by land, sea and air. Upon their arrival I was notified that all had arrived in good condition and very shortly afterward they all kindled well. This proved my point that hamsters do not mind travelling. Many owners take their pets with them on holidays in trailers and they return to say how well the hamster enjoyed itself.

A light gray long-haired female hamster. When breeding hamsters, remember that it takes quality to beget quality.

Exhibiting Hamsters

According to the National Hamster Council rules, judges look for, above all, a hamster of good size with a broad, rounded skull on a large head and with a short, blunt unratlike face. The eyes should be bold, large, prominent, and set well apart. The ears should be large, set well apart, and upstanding when the hamster is awake. The fur should be soft, short and dense, except in the case of long-haired hamsters. In the long-haired variety, the fur should be long, soft and fine in texture.

These, then, are the things to aim for when trying to breed winners. You may have noticed that I use the phrase "trying to breed winners." The number of people I have met who say that they are going to breed show animals amuses me. I have been trying for over thirty years and have bred quite a good number of winners, I suppose, in my time. Most of those winners have been given away to club members or kept as winner-

Below: *A chocolate roan female hamster.* **Opposite:** *A young golden male hamster.*

breeding stock.

In my younger days I had a team of winning hamsters, six in number; one white, one cream, one golden (all males) and one golden piebald female, all bred by myself. The remaining two colors I can not recall. This team I sent by train to the Yorkshire Hamster Club Show; from there it was sent to the Midland Hamster Club, who sent it to the Southern Hamster Club Show. The piebald female, bred from stock that I imported from the United States, won best in show two years in a row after travelling some two thousand miles back and forth. She was a champion; I have never seen a hamster win best in show two years running before or since that hamster did. This is one of the joys of exhibiting; it is useless to sit back and think you have some winners—because you have not—they stay in tip-top show condition for only a short time. So, you must breed some more hamsters that are like, or better than, those that have just faded away.

A long-haired dark gray male hamster. This animal is two months old, and its adult coat is just beginning to grow.

A gray dominant spot female and a cinnamon dominant spot female hamster.

HAMSTER SHOWS

1) There are National Hamster Council Shows that are run by an affiliated club for the benefit of the N.H.C.

2) Open shows are shows arranged by mutual agreement between secretaries of clubs affiliated with the N.H.C.

3) Club shows are run primarily for the member of the club holding the show.

4) Handstock shows are those to which all exhibits are brought by the exhibitors, as the title implies. Railstock is not accepted.

5) Sweepstakes shows are those at which the prize monies paid are percentages of the total entry fees for each class.

At all of these shows, in fact, at every show held under N.H.C.

Rules, all of the exhibits must be caged in standard show pens, particulars on which are given in the N.H.C. handbook. Upon joining a club affiliated to the National Hamster Council, members are given a handbook that states: "No person may touch an exhibit or show pen, etc. . .," while rule number 31 states: "No exhibitor may handle or indicate his or her exhibit during the judging." All these rules protect the owner as well as the hamster.

The National Hamster Council has regulations for setting up new show standards, amending them to bring them up to date and for the recognition of new varieties.

I have the honor of presiding at all N.H.C. meetings so far held in the United Kingdom. The first meeting was held in Boston, Linc. (U.K.), and has always been referred to as the "Boston Tea Party"—not much of a tea party, but it lasted all night.

Before rushing in to show your

A group of female hamsters: a golden dominant spot, a light gray tortoiseshell, a golden tortoiseshell, and a satinized dominant spot.

A white-bellied tortoiseshell hamster. The number of hamster varieties available continues to grow as breeders create new and fascinating strains.

hamsters, take my advice and visit a few of the shows that are held under N.H.C. rules. Here you will see hamsters shown in standard show pens that are designed to show off the exhibits at their best. You will also meet members, who, like yourself, are interested in exhibiting hamsters. It is at these shows that you can and will learn more about show hamsters than any book will be able to tell you. Once you have been to a show I am sure that it will be the first of many more visits. Make yourself known to club officials who will be glad to put you in touch with exhibitors and breeders that are present. They will be only too pleased to let you see their stock and to chat with you about their animals.

Exhibiting Hamsters

STANDARDS

Judging these days is done on the points system, as follows:

Color and Markings	40 points
Type	20 points
Fur	15 points
Size	10 points
Condition	10 points
Eyes and Ears	5 points
Total	100

General Body Type

The whole body shall be cobby and broad. The head to be well set, short nosed and unratlike. The fur shall be soft, dense and short, with good belly fur. Size of the hamster to be as large as possible without being fat, making allowance for the sex (females being generally larger).

A rust satin hamster. Although rust hamsters look similar to cinnamon hamsters, they are a different mutation altogether.

A cream male hamster. Note the dark ears on this specimen; their color matches the standard's requirement for ear color in the black-eyed cream variety.

Condition

The animal shall be in a fit condition, alert and easy to handle. The body to be firm with no surplus fat. The coat to be clean, unsoiled and shiny.

Eyes and Ears

Both eyes and ears should be large, prominent and set well apart.

Penalties

Disease—disqualification
Excess fat—minus 15 points
Sores, wounds or scars—minus 10 points maximum
Hamsters shown in dirty or stained pens—minus 10 points maximum

Syrian Hamster Varieties

Dark Golden

Rich mahogany red with black ticking, slate-gray undercoat. Belly fur, crescents and throat as white as possible.

Ears—black
Eyes—black

Black-eyed Cream

Discovered in Yorkshire (U.K.) in 1951.

Whole body fur to be peach colored throughout, no shading or marking.

Ears—very dark gray, nearly black
Eyes—jet black

Red-eyed Cream

Very fertile. Not to be confused with ruby-eyed stock.

More rufous than black-eyed cream, even in color throughout, with no fading.

Ears—flesh colored
Eyes—red (not ruby)

Ruby-eyed Cream

The body fur throughout to be pastel pinkish cream without shading.

Ears—flesh colored
Eyes—ruby

Ruby-eyed Fawn

The whole body to be a clean bright fawn, with pale gray undercoat, belly fur white.

Ears—pale gray
Eyes—ruby

Cinnamon

The body fur to be cinnamon orange on top with blue/gray undercoat. Belly fur white as possible. Flashes cinnamon brown.

Ears—cinnamon brown
Eyes—claret red

Black-eyed White

Body fur to be pure white to the roots.

Ears—flesh colored (spotted ears will lose points)
Eyes—jet black

Dark-eared Albino

The body fur shall be pure white.

Ears—very dary gray, nearly black
Eyes—bright clear pink in color darkening with age

Flesh-eared Albino

Body fur to be pure white (unstained)

Ears—almost colorless
Eyes—pink as albino mice, etc.
(Only mate pure strains to avoid color change)

Sepia

Body fur to be light tawny beige, lightly ticked with dark guard (long) hairs. Pale gray undercoat.

Belly fur and crescents as white as possible.

Ears—dark gray
Eyes—black

Opposite: *Any hamster that is to be exhibited must be in perfect health in addition to meeting the standard's description.*

A light gray satinized tortoiseshell hamster.

Tortoiseshell and White

Whole body fur to be colored, yellow and white patches.

Ears—color as stipulated for the full colored variety

Eyes—color as stipulated for the full color variety

This mutation was discovered by me here on the farm in 1962. The hamsters were golden with yellow patches on them, but later were produced with small yellow spots the size of a pea. After many matings, the size of these spots was increased. By introducing banded stock we then produced tortoiseshell and whites. Although the inclination is to call these tortoiseshell, this is not correct. In line with other small animal fanciers, we applied for the standard to be called "tortoiseshell and white." They are accepted on the show bench in all standard colors today: golden tortoiseshell and white; cinnamon tortoiseshell and white; gray tortoiseshell and white and so on.

Piebald Tortoiseshell

The whole body fur shall be a standard color (show standard) with even size patches of color spread evenly over the whole white body fur. The white areas to be pure white to the roots.

Ears—color as stipulated for the full color variety, also partly or entirely flesh colored.

Eyes—as stipulated for the full color variety, also ruby eye or eyes permissible

A pair of piebald hamsters.

Syrian Hamster Varieties

Honey

Body fur shall be entirely honey colored (the color of solidified honey) to the roots. Crescents and belly fur light honey.

Ears and flashes—honey gray
Eyes—claret red

This color was produced by me in 1964, and a show standard approved by the N.H.C. in 1966.

White Band

Body fur shall be as any standard color variety superimposed by a white band around the middle; approximately one third of the body shall be a clearly defined clean cut white band.

Ears—generally mottled, but may be as in full colored variety.
Eyes—as full colored variety

First discovered in U.S.A., imported to U.K. in 1958.

Satin

Color, type, etc. as for the full

A golden umbrous banded female hamster.

A long-haired satinized cream female hamster.

color variety, allowing for increase in color through satinization. The coat shall be extremely fine and glossy, giving a satin sheen.

Note: Under *no* circumstances should two satins be mated together or double satinization will result which gives a very unpleasant appearance to the coat. *At all times mate satin to non-satin.*

Gray

The top coat shall be dark gray ticked with black and a band of pearly gray should be seen on parting the fur. The base of the fur shall be pale gray, almost white. Chest band dark gray. Cheek flashes deeply pigmented and crisply defined, bordered by white crescents.

Ears—very dark gray, nearly black

Eyes—black

To breed a very dark gray, mate a dark golden to gray—being dominant, the litter would have some golden (not carrying gray at all), some very dark gray. If two grays are mated together all the youngsters would be gray but lighter in color. Each time a generation was mated together they would become lighter and lighter in color.

Beige

The top coat shall be beige (as the beige chinchilla), carried well down into the fur. The belly fur shall be pale beige, the crescents very pale beige.

Ears—dark beige

Eyes—black

Blonde

The whole coat shall be blonde in color carried well down into

A long-haired roan female hamster. Long-haired hamsters may require some grooming in order to keep their coats in show condition.

Profile of a long-haired satinized dove male hamster.

the fur.

Ears—flesh colored

Eyes—very dark ruby red, almost black

Other colors include:
Tortoiseshell

All of the self colors can be bred in tortoiseshell, such as gray tortoiseshell, cinnamon tortoiseshell, and also in satin-coated, rex-coated, and long-haired.

At the present the National Hamster Council does not have a standard for the rex (those with coats like the rex-coated rabbit). The guard hairs on the rex are quite short, making the plush-like fur stand up like the pile on a carpet.

Mosaics

While there is no N.H.C. standard for mosaics, they can be bred in all sorts of colors. At

Breeders are attempting to create a golden-faced hamster. This variety would have a golden face with a clear white coat.

the time of this writing, we have on the farm cream mosaics, black-eyed white mosaics, dark-eared white mosaics and just one male satin black-eyed cream mosaic long-haired.

What about the whites? As white is not a color, we mention it now. The black-eyed white, having some pigment to make it colored, is included in the list. We could have mentioned the dark-eared white but this is not truly a colored animal. There are many types of albinos that can be bred, and also eyeless whites.

Guinea-Gold

The whole coat shall be guinea-gold in color, with no

dark guard hairs. Belly fur creamy gold. Crescents and collar dark guinea-gold.
  Ears—black
  Eyes—black

Long-haired Hamsters

Color, type, etc. as for the full color variety. The coat shall be as long as possible, soft and silky to the touch with no matting or signs of matting being cut or pulled out, allowance being made for sex (only the males having the long skirt).

The beige was produced by me at the farm in 1971, from the new gray. The blonde was produced by me in 1973 from the new gray. Recognition of these three varieties was given by the National Hamster Council in 1975. (At all times the color of eyes and ears given refers to the adult hamster.) Mention of standards, show standards, colors, etc. refer to those recognized by the National Hamster Council.

A mosaic black-eyed white. The mosaic variety was created from piebald hamsters. However, a standard for this variety has not yet been written.

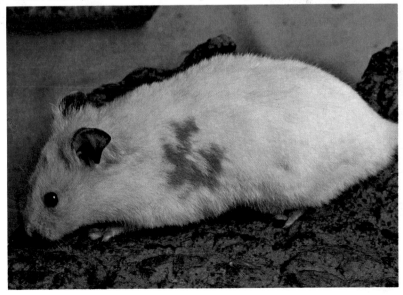

Diseases and Ailments

Bad management can and will determine the life of your hamster but most hamsters die of old age. It is wise to learn as much as you can about them so that you will know that you are not responsible for their deaths.

Should your hamster appear to be ill, do not hesitate to take it to a qualified veterinarian. Self-doctoring is likely to do more harm than good. Giving it whiskey or brandy, thinking it will do some good, will more than likely kill it.

Small Cuts, Skin Damage

These are usually taken care of by your hamster himself. Hamsters are wonderful little healers and it is amazing how quickly they will get back to normal by washing and cleaning the damaged parts themselves. I have seen a pregnant hamster lose a leg a few days before kindling and then go on to rear a good litter with no trouble at all. The leg healed up in four days and the skin and fur grew within fourteen days. You would never notice the leg was missing.

Teeth

A healthy hamster's teeth should not be white but tinted brown. They grow long, but this is quite normal. If you keep a piece of hard dog biscuit in your hamster's cage for it to gnaw on, its teeth should not require any further attention. Should your

hamster have one of its teeth broken off, the tooth can easily be cut down a little with a pair of nail scissors.

Wet Tail

This dreaded disease is a killer for hamsters. Little is known about this highly infectious disease except that it is caused by a tapeworm and usually proves to be fatal. Symptoms of this disease are: loss of sheen, loss of clean appearance, ears laying down, loss of appetite, a jelly-like fluid coming from the vent.

Wet tail is exactly as its name implies—a very wet tail. This is followed by a complete loss of appetite, listlessness and a bad temper, as a rule. Your veterinarian may be able to save your hamster's life if you take it for medical attention in time, but death usually occurs from this disease within a few days. Your veterinarian has the required medicines that may give your hamster a chance to live.

After taking your infected hamster to the veterinarian, you

Opposite: *A healthy hamster will have bright eyes and a shiny coat. If your hamster appears to be getting sick, take it to the veterinarian immediately.*

Diseases and Ailments

must stop the spread of infection by isolating each hamster and keeping them far apart, in another room if possible. All suspect stock should be watched very carefully for any of the above symptoms. Clean out the infected cage, burn its contents and disinfect it with a good disinfectant. All food and water containers should be discarded; disinfect all tools that you use and clean your hands thoroughly.

Always tend to the well stock before the sick ones. By doing this, there will be less chances of spreading the infection to the well hamsters. Should you save one of your hamsters that could have had wet tail it would be most unwise to use that hamster

A smoke pearl hamster. Cleanliness will go a long way in preventing illness in your hamster.

A group of blue hamsters. Once you suspect that a hamster is sick, move its cage away from those of your other hamsters.

for breeding.

Diarrhea

This should not be confused with wet tail. It is caused by incorrect diet, by eating foods that have been contaminated by rats, dogs, cats, mice, birds and chemical sprays. Diarrhea is more likely to be a sign that something is wrong, such as a severe stomach upset or even a blockage. Consult your veterinarian and he will be able to tell you what is wrong with your hamster.

Baldness

Loss of fur in old hamsters is quite normal. If your hamsters lose fur when they are five months old or younger, consult your veterinarian. As a rule, when hamsters are from ten to

Diseases and Ailments

twelve months old they will begin to lose fur from the rump on upwards. This can be helped by giving your hamster a yeast tablet that has been powdered along with one of its favorite tid-bits. Within reason this cannot be overdone as the body will only take the amount of yeast that it needs and discard the rest.

Fleas and Lice

It is not unusual for your hamster to have either of these—they can be passed on from cats, dogs, rats and mice. If you suspect that your hamster has either of these, sprinkle any

A long-haired paled-eared albino male hamster.

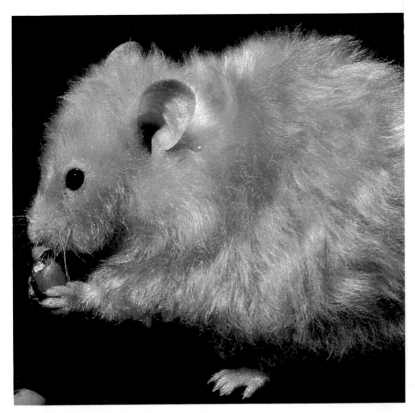

A red-eyed cream satinized rex angora hamster.

type of flea powder around the nest every four days. Change the complete bedding before another application so that you will be able to stop any eggs from hatching in the cage.

Mastitis

Hard lumps in the mammae indicate mastitis. You should

consult a veterinarian at once.

Hip Spots

These two spots, one on each side of the hips, show up when your hamster has been washing them. They are quite normal and you should not interfere with them. In the wild state these spots are used to mark out the

Diseases and Ailments

hamster's domain; they are really scent spots. Both sexes have these spots that secrete a scented fluid and are so placed that they would easily mark both sides of the burrow, warning off any intruders.

Over the years I have noticed that these spots are becoming less noticeable; at no time have I been able to smell the scent that is given off, although my collie has been able to. Do not bother with these spots at all; putting ointments on them will do more harm than good.

If he is given good food, clean surroundings, and sufficient attention, your hamster will most likely remain very healthy throughout his life.

Index

Hamsters
KW-015